MW01600662

Summary of From Strength to Strength

By

Arthur C. Brooks

Finding Success, Happiness, and Deep Purpose in
the Second Half of Life

Justin Reese

NOTE TO READERS

This is an unofficial summary & analysis of Arthur C. Brooks's "From Strength to Strength: Finding Success, Happiness, and Deep Purpose in the Second Half of Life" designed to enrich your reading experience. Buy the original book Here

DISCLAIMER

Contents

INTRODUCTION

The Man on the Plane Who Changed My Life

Bob Greene eavesdropped on a plane conversation from Los Angeles to Washington. Bob Greene's professional life was going pretty well, but he wasn't particularly satisfied or happy. He wondered if he could get off the hamster wheel of success and accept inevitable professional decline. Greene decided to turn his future from a matter of dread to an opportunity for progress. Michael Wolraich: I came to call this the striver's curse: people who strive to be excellent at what they do often wind up finding their successes terrifying.

The secrets I found were available to anyone with a will to live a life of joy and purpose. You can transcend decline by finding a new kind of success, better than what the world promises and not a source of neurosis and addiction. I ask you not to deny your weaknesses but rather to embrace them defenselessly. It takes great effort to accept ideas that might have seemed crazy before.

CHAPTER 1

Your Professional Decline Is Coming (Much) Sooner Than You Think

Charles Darwin changed our understanding of biology completely and permanently. He died considering his career to be a disappointment. His magnum opus and crowning achievement, On the Origin of Species, was published in 1859. The theory of evolution made him into a household name and changed science forever. In his last years, Charles Darwin became increasingly unhappy about his life, seeing his work as unsatisfying, unsatisfactory, and unoriginal.

I'd like to tell you that Darwin's unhappiness in old age was as rare as his achievements, but that's not true. The average American dies six years before entering old age. In almost every high-skill profession, decline sets in sometime between one's late thirties and early fifties. The more accomplished one is at the peak of one's career, the more pronounced decline seems. Jones and his co-authors looked at data on researchers in physics, chemistry, medicine and other fields who had highly cited work.

Even by the most optimistic estimates, only about 5 percent of founders are over sixty. Peak performance is thirty-five to forty-four for equipment-service engineers and office workers. The age-related decline among air-traffic controllers is so sharp that the mandatory retirement age is fifty-six. In surveys, classical musicians report that peak performance occurs in one's thirties. If you are a geologist, your peak will tend to come closer to fifty-four.

Younger players groan over older players with tenure who hang around long after they've lost their edge. My dream was to join a top symphony orchestra in a few years and then become a soloist. But as I got older, my playing deteriorated and I couldn't get back to where I had been. When I was 21, I abandoned my musical aspirations and started a PhD in economics. After finishing my studies, I became a university professor engaged in social science research and teaching.

But I still thought every day about my beloved career as a musician. One theory is that intelligence decreases with age, but research shows the opposite is true. The prefrontal cortex, the part of the brain behind your forehead, changes as we age. Older adults can enhance their cognitive effectiveness by turning off their phones and going quiet, researchers show. By the time you are fifty, your brain is as crowded with information as the New York Public Library.

Some people deal with decline fairly well. Take the case of Paul Dirac, whose most important work and productive years were in his twenties and early thirties. After World War II, Nobel-winning chemist Linus Pauling turned his attention to antinuclear crusading. Pauling's hunger for relevance led him to promote faddish, quasi-scientific ideas. He became obsessed with his own theory that vitamins could cure a host of diseases and massively extend life.

Bob Greene says he's seen himself through the eyes of his colleagues over the years. From his outsider's view it looked like a weariness had set in. The cost of lost sleep or too much travel takes a toll on our bodies, and we used to rebound quickly. The agony of decline is directly related to prestige previously achieved, and to one's emotional attachment to that prestige. In my profession, go earn tenure and you will be all set.

But if you attain excellence and are deeply invested in it, you can feel pretty irrelevant when you inevitably fall from those heights. He argues that we can't store up our glories and enjoy them when they are long past as we did in the past with athletes, for example. When it comes to the enviable skills that made you successful, you can expect significant decline to come as soon as your thirties or as late as your fifties.

CHAPTER 2

The Second Curve

As we age, there are some specific ways in which we naturally get smarter and more skillful. The trick to improving as we age is to understand, develop, and practice these new strengths. If you can understand this, you can transform decline into incredible new success. Psychologist Raymond Cattell posited that there are two types of intelligence that people possess, but at greater abundance at different points in life. The first is fluid intelligence, and the second is raw smarts, which researchers find is associated with both reading and mathematical ability.

Fluid intelligence is the ability to learn quickly and solve hard problems. When you are young, you have raw smarts; when you are old, wisdom, Cattell's theory says. If your career relies solely on fluid intelligence, it's true that you will peak and decline pretty early.

But if your career requires crystallized intelligence, your peak will come later. And if you can go from one type to the other, then you have cracked the code.

Older professors take up faculty lines that could be used to hire young scholars, authors say. The question is how to adjust their work portfolio toward teaching without loss of professional status. Cicero wrote that the old should be dedicated to service, not goofing off. Cicero was assassinated at the age of sixty-three for his less than politically correct ideas. The pinnacle of crystallized intelligence, he was a teacher with his dying breath.

Alex Castellanos argues that there is a second wave of success that favors people who are older. They can also offer wisdom that only comes with years in the school of hard knocks. Michael Wolraich's new book, Older is Best, looks at why older people are happiest and most satisfied in their fifties, sixties, and seventies. He interviewed a fifty-eight-year-old actuary and a television journalist who were retiring to become teachers. He wrote more than 1,000 compositions for every instrumentation of his day.

Bach fathered twenty children, seven by his beloved first wife Maria Barbara and 13 by his second wife Anna Magdalena. Johannes S. Bach's son C. P. E. was considered one of the greatest composers of the baroque era. Mozart said, "Bach is the father, we are the children," referring to C.P.

E., not J. S. J. S. Bach died working on his master text. The manuscript for his Contrapunctus 14 from The Art of Fugue stops midmeasure. C. P. E.

added these words: "Über dieser Fuge .. ist der Verfasser gestorben". Bach's exemplary life shows that his calling was molded perfectly to his changing skills, and as such was filled with joy, love, and service to others. Let's take Brahms's advice not just for music, but study Bach to improve our lives as well. In the book, I will show you how to jump from what rewards fluid intelligence to crystallized intelligence. Develop your relationships, start your spiritual journey, and embrace your weaknesses. Get old sharing the things you believe are most important with the people who matter most to you.

CHAPTER 3

Kick Your Success Addiction

Greene talks with a woman who says she's not been happy for many years. She says she would prefer to be "special rather than happy". A financier felt like every hour of work was giving her less than the last, and not just less happiness but less power and prestige, too. She had traded herself for a symbol of herself, you might say. In this chapter, we examine self-objectification, workaholism, and success addiction.

But then I thought back to a friend who struggled with alcoholism and drug addiction. He told me that he was miserable all the time because he cared more about being high than being happy. "Workaholics" are caught in a vicious cycle of fear and loneliness. Fear feeds fear; loneliness feeds workaholism. Workaholics believe they have to work more than others to maintain their astronomical productivity.

The work crowds out relationships and outside activities, leaving little else. Workaholics have many of the same patterns of behavior and estrangement with their spouses as alcoholics. Some forgo marriage for their careers, knowing full well that a good marriage is more satisfying than any job. What workaholics crave isn't work per se; it is success. They kill themselves working for money, power, and prestige because these are forms of approval, applause, and compliments.

The thrill of success blots out the blackness of "normal" life. To be noticed, to achieve specialness, to be noticed doesn't come cheap. Apart from a few reality TV stars and accidental celebrities, success is brutal work and takes sacrifices. The high only lasts a day or two, and then it's on to the next success hit. The moral case against objectifying others is fairly straightforward.

It starts to get more complicated when the objectifier and the one being objectified are the same person. In the case of physical self-objectification, studies show that it leads to depression and self-hatred. Self-objectification leads to a sense of invisibility and lack of autonomy, as well as eating disorders and depression. It also lowers competence in normal, everyday tasks. We become Marx's heartless work overlord to ourselves, cracking the whip mercilessly.

Love and fun are sacrificed for another day of work. In almost all philosophical traditions, pride is a deadly vice that rots a person from the inside out. Buddhists use the word māna to describe an inflated mind that disregards others in favor of the self and leads to one's own suffering. Fear animates all success addicts. Expert: People who fear failure are motivated less by the possibility of winning and more by their fear of messing up.

Success addicts confess that they feel like losers when they see someone else who is yet more successful. The drive to achieve worldly success for positional reasons can easily become an obsessive passion. Getting and staying famous is a miserable combination of boredom and terror. Emily Dickinson captured this drudgery in her poem "I'm Nobody!". Researchers have found that social comparison lowers our happiness.

To quit is to lose intimacy with others, and the prospect of never feeling good again. Are you a success addict? If you define your self-worth in terms of your job title or professional position, you're probably an addict. He says the first step in recovery from an addiction is admitting you have a problem and that you want to be happy. "From the fear of being humiliated, deliver me, Master," he implores.

Inspired by this, I have a little litany that I use when I find myself becoming chained to addictions. The point is to name your addictions and state your desire to be free. As you get older, you might find that a lot of the things in your life were really just to build up your image. Some of these are physical trophies, "positional goods" that show you are a big deal to the world. Others are social media followers, or famous friends, or living in a cool place.

CHAPTER 4

Start Chipping Away

Taiwan's National Palace Museum houses arguably the greatest collection of Chinese art and artifacts in the world. The museum's permanent collection contains more than seven thousand items that date from the Neolithic period to the early 20th century. A tour quickly becomes a forced march past pots, prints, and carved pieces of stone without guidance. In the West, success and happiness come by avoiding losses and accumulating more stuff. Eastern philosophy warns that this acquisitiveness leads to materialism and vanity.

As we age, we shouldn't accumulate more to represent ourselves but rather strip things away to find our true selves. Bob Greene's happiest days are those that start out like an empty canvas, waiting to be filled with ideas and creative interactions. Instead of adding more and more to our lives, we need to understand why this doesn't work and then start taking things away. This is the "bucket list" strategy. When Thomas Aquinas could not find a professional success, he turned to his bucket list.

He bought houses, cars, art, and other items as a substitute for the success he craved. Francesco Aquino's life was a struggle against the idols of money, power, pleasure and honor. Even if you are not a religious believer, his list rings true as the idols that attract us. The idols leave us dissatisfied because they are not what we need as complete persons. Thomas Aquinas argued that attachment, power, pleasure and honor are inadequate for delivering what our hearts desire.

Thomas didn't just pontificate about this; he lived it. He attained true greatness only by chipping away the world's rewards to find his essential self. Siddhartha lived a life of poverty, renouncing all pleasures, starving himself, and exposing himself to pain. He eventually realized that release from suffering comes not from renunciation of the things of the world, but from release from attachment. Suffering can be defeated by eliminating craving, desire, and attachment for worldly things.

Neither Thomas nor the Buddha argued that there is something inherently evil about worldly rewards. The only solution to this problem is to shed my attachments and redefine my desires, Mahayana Buddhism says. Satisfaction is defined by equation: Satisfaction = Getting what you want - for a couple of days at most. "Homeostasis" is the natural tendency for all living systems to maintain stable conditions in order to survive. It explains how drugs and alcohol work, and why addicts pine for that first-time feeling.

As a child, the first drink of alcohol gave you a huge, awesome buzz, and when it wears off you feel terrible. Addiction is basically a maladaptation of homeostasis, in which the brain becomes very adept at dealing with constant onslaughts to its equilibrium. Satisfaction = Continually getting what you want, with the carrot dangled in front of you is the fleeting feeling that you've made it. Successful people often keep working to increase their wealth, accumulating far beyond anything they could possibly spend and more than they want to bequeath. When we are talking about satisfaction from a success, there's another element to consider: success is all relative.

The small rush of pleasure we get from being envied by others one minute is swallowed up by the unhappiness from having less than someone else the next. Daniel Kahneman's theory of prospect theory explains why we hate disappointment so much. People are more affected emotionally by losing something than gaining the same thing. Loss aversion makes perfect evolutionary sense, as humans lived on edge of starvation in pre-industrial times when gain was potentially lethal. Dopamine, the neurotransmitter of pleasure behind nearly all addictive behaviors, is excreted in response to thoughts about buying new things.

Psychologist Carl Jung noted that "what is a normal goal to a young person becomes a neurotic hindrance in old age". The futility of attaining satisfaction is one of the reasons that professional decline is so painful. As you increase your haves without managing your wants, your wants will proliferate and sprawl. You can easily be less and less satisfied as you move up the success ladder. Carol Costello: The Mercedes brings her less satisfaction at age fifty than the Chevy did at age thirty.

Because now she wants a Ferrari. She doesn't even know what's going on—she always just gets back on the treadmill and starts running. If you are ready to manage your wants, the first step is to ask what exactly needs chipping away. The bestselling author and speaker Simon Sinek always gives people in search of true success in work and life the advice that they need to find their why.

CHAPTER 5
Ponder Your Death

Greene argues that if you live to work, your fear of decline is actually a type of fear of death. Work is your identity, and your professional ability and achievement are your mortality. Existential fear is not the stuff of biologists, but of philosophers. The fear of decline involves this same fear of nonexistence. If my existence in relation to others is defined by my professional standing, my decline will effectively erase me.

Cambridge University philosopher Stephen Cave calls this the "mortality paradox". When Walt Disney was a boy, an owl entered his dreams and haunted him for years. It created in him a morbid fear of death that colored his professional and personal life. Virtually every one of his most famous films focused on the subject from Snow White to Pinocchio. Bob Greene: Do you really want to go on forever?

He says in Gulliver's Travels, a group of people are born immortal but age and become senile. Greene: If you live to work, you might give the same answer if someone asks, "How's work?". In real life, we try to engineer a professional legacy, but people forget you. Stoic Marcus Aurelius says our efforts at posterity always fail, and thus are not worth pursuing. If you spend time thinking about and working on your legacy, you are already done.

Your eulogy virtues are what you really would want people to talk about at your funeral. The right way to think about your legacy will help you live better right now. What gives you more satisfaction, an extra hour at work or an hour helping someone in need? Leo Tolstoy says to live in such a way as to be always ready to die. Focus on mindfulness helps us make the decisions that truly expose our best selves.

Exposure therapy has been firmly established as the best way to take on fears and phobias. Contemplating death can even make life more meaningful, writes Julian Zelizer. Remembering that life won't last forever makes us enjoy it all the more today. Buddhist monks practice a meditation called maranasati (mindfulness of death). In it, the practitioner imagines nine states of his or her own dead body: swollen corpse, blue and festering, being eaten by scavengers and worms, blood-smeared bones without flesh but held together with tendons.

The samurai leader snarls at the monks, "Don't you see that I am the sort of man who could run you through without batting an eye?". With decline, you don't have to experience it alone. But many people do decline alone: on their way up they have let relationships wither.

CHAPTER 6

Cultivate Your Aspen Grove

Aspen is the largest living organism in the world; one stand of aspens in Utah spans 106 acres and weighs 6 million kilograms. Each individual tree forms part of an enormous root system. The redwood tree, which can grow to 275 feet tall, has remarkably shallow roots. Buddhism teaches that the "self" is an illusion and that we are all intertwined. Creating an isolated self is dangerous and damaging because it is unnatural.

Many strivers have spent their adult lives under the illusion of their solitariness and now suffer the result. In this week's Daily Discussion, we look back at the Harvard Study of Adult Development. Fewer than sixty of the original 268 men are still alive, and the study is now tracking children and grandchildren of the first generation. The best off were called "Happy-Well," who enjoyed six dimensions of good physical health and high life satisfaction. The "Sad-Sick" were below average in physical health, mental health and life satisfaction.

Loneliness is the experience of emotional and social isolation. It has the weird property of being utterly ubiquitous yet feeling completely unique. Some people are happiest by themselves, as long as they have healthy social and emotional connections. Research shows that good relationships keep us happier and healthier. In terms of health outcomes, loneliness is comparable to smoking fifteen cigarettes per day and is worse than obesity.

Lonely people tend toward high-calorie, high-fat diets and lead more sedentary lives. Loneliness is driving up costs for health care companies. Bob Greene: Successful, upwardly mobile people are most prone to suffering when their skills start to decline. Greene: Loneliness is a special malady for people who have enjoyed a lot of worldly success. The top two loneliest professions are lawyers and doctors, according to Harvard Business Review.

Anthony Bourdain suffered from workaholism and what one author called his "unfathomable loneliness". Success-addicted workaholics leave little room for friends or family. People at the top often miss out on true workplace friendships, he says. The top spot for negative interactions? No one wants to hang around with the lonely boss.

Successful people are lonely in a crowd because their success requires manipulation and persuasion. As such, they objectify subordinates every bit as much as subordinates objectify them. The Harvard Study data shows that marriage accounts for only 2 percent of subjective well-being later in life. The secret to happiness isn't falling in love; it's staying in love. Psychologists call it "companionate love," which is based less on passionate highs and lows and more on stable affection.

Best friends get enjoyment, satisfaction, and meaning from each other's company. President Calvin Coolidge and his wife, Grace, famously had such a friendship. In 2004, a survey found that for men and women, the happiness-maximizing number of sexual partners is 1. Having a spouse as your one and only close friend is imprudent, says author Barbara Ehrenreich. Marriage bonds are more emotionally important to men as they age, she argues.

Older women tend to have larger, denser, supportive friend networks than men. I wanted my independence. It was important to me to have a certain amount of separation, not from bitterness but because I wanted to build my own life. Author's relationship with his kids is great, but they are focused on their lives, not mine.

Aristotle's "friendship ladder" gives three levels of friendship, from lowest to highest.

At the bottom are friendships based on utility: instrumental friends who help each other achieve something else. Aristotle's "perfect friendship" is based on willing each other's well-being and a shared love for something virtuous. If you haven't talked to your real friends in a long time, you might not have cultivated real friendships. One of the great markers for happiness is being able to name a few authentic, close friends. The number of real friends needs to be more than zero and more than just your spouse.

Love and friendships are enormously time-consuming, it's true. They crowd out all kinds of other things, like work. If you are displaying workaholic behavior, no amount of advice about making friends will help. You need to address the workaholism problem before anything else.

CHAPTER 7

Start Your *Vanaprastha*

"Acharya" ("Teacher") is Sri Nochur Venkataraman, a spiritual teacher in south India. Unlike many of the wealth- and fame-seeking guru-entrepreneurs in India, Acharya is not rich, seeks no media presence, and has never been to the West. He has taught that a proper life must be lived in four distinct stages, or ashramas. Ashramas should ideally last twenty-five years each. Vanaprastha is the stage at which we purposively pull back from our old personal and professional duties, becoming more devoted to spirituality and deep wisdom.

The goal of the last phase of life is to drink from the chalice of life's deepest secrets. Many of us suffer from psychoprofessional gravitation as a result of workaholics and success addicts. The decline in fluid intelligence is a sign that it is time not to rage, but to scale up crystallized intelligence and share it with others. Faith, religion, spirituality, or perhaps just interest in the transcendent commonly grows in our hearts as we move into middle adulthood. For many, the metaphysical begins to feel real as we get older.

Research shows that religious and spiritual adults are generally happier and suffer less depression. When you spend serious time and effort focused on transcendental things, it puts your little world into proper context and takes the focus off yourself. Faith forces me into the cosmos, to consider the source of truth, the origin of life, and the good of others. In particular, we examine the personal journey of J. S. Bach, who wrote music to sanctify his work for the glory of God and the service of others.

When I met Ester, I fell in love with her, but we didn't speak a word of the same language. Acharya's lessons about vanaprastha greatly expanded my consciousness. Ester leads me down the path of righteousness; she takes me every single day to Mass. Henry Wadsworth Longfellow imagines Nicademus as a man caught between old beliefs and new ones that attract him. Unlike many followers, he takes responsibility for Jesus's body and preserves it.

He is now clearly "all in," devoted to Jesus even after the Master's death. Perhaps his transformation has lessons for you. The key is to subtly shift your self from "none" to "none right now" or, perhaps, "none but open to suggestion". Many opponents of religion attack it by appealing to childhood memories that we should logically leave behind. When spiritual urges arise, the appropriate course of action is not to cross-reference them to ideas we had as children.

Spirituality is a huge time imposition. As such, many people craving faith simply never find the time or never devote enough effort. You must make the time by scheduling your meditation, prayer, reading, and practice. For many, what's needed is simply an excuse to get started. In the Hindu tradition, the "wanderer," often a penniless mendicant, is held in reverence.

For Catholics, there is the Camino de Santiago, or Way of Saint James, across northern Spain. The number of pilgrims has risen from 145,877 in 2009 to 347,578 in 2019. The Camino is a form of extended walking meditation, a practice in many traditions. The walk becomes a long piece of music, neither lags nor hurries, which brings a sense of ease. Fulfillment cannot come when the present moment is little more than a struggle to bear in order to attain the future.

One day is dedicated to focusing in prayer or meditation on the good of another. The walking meditation creates a sense of love and compassion for the objects of each intention, and finishes with a concrete resolution.

CHAPTER 8

Make Your Weakness Your Strength

Paul is considered the inventor of Christianity as an organized religion. He organized the work of a messianic itinerant preacher into a body of coherent theology. Paul's entrepreneurial secret? Liking "to be weak, for Christ's sake, I delight in weaknesses," he wrote. Paul's letters suggest that he suffered from temporal lobe epilepsy, which would explain his ecstatic personal experiences such as being "caught up to paradise," and seeing visions.

This could also explain the flash of light he experienced on the road to Damascus, followed by temporary blindness. Frida Ghitis: "The true master uses the inevitable failures, including the declines, as a source of deep human connection". Ghitis studied abroad and got her undergraduate degree by distance learning. She left university teaching to become president of a think tank; she wrote an article about nontraditional education. Bob Greene: Elite credentials don't make you relatable; they are a barrier to deep human connection.

He says Saint Paul saw his earthly work as a failure, destined to be forgotten. Greene: If you want to connect with someone, your strengths and worldly successes won't cut it. Paul's words of sadness and suffering at the end of his life magnetized the Christian faith for the ages. He wrote to the Corinthian church "out of great distress and anguish of heart and with many tears" The evidence is overwhelming that defenselessness enhances life success. Stephen Colbert's father, brothers were killed in a plane crash when he was ten years old.

The key is finding meaning in the suffering and sharing that meaning with others. This flies in the face of established wisdom that trauma from pain and loss is always harmful to a person, says author David Frum. Frida Ghitis: Many of the most meaningful experiences in life are quite painful. Exposure to negative emotions make us stronger for when there is a true crisis, she says. Research shows that stress inoculation training is effective in creating emotional resilience, Ghitis writes.

For a long time after he could barely hear, he insisted on performing on the piano, with worse and worse results. He would bang the keys so hard that he ruined pianos. In the last decade of Beethoven's life, his deafness was complete. That meant the end of his compositional career, right? During that period he wrote music that would define his unique style and give him a legacy as one of the greatest composers.

To see weakness as purely negative is a mistake. Stop hiding it, and don't resist it. When you are honest and humble about your weaknesses, you will be more comfortable in your own skin. And you can finally relax without worrying about being exposed as less than people think you are. If you are reluctant to embrace your weaknesses, start by imagining the peace in your heart from no longer pretending you are not weak.

Visualize others drawn to you as a person of authenticity, defenseless and unafraid. See how they relax around you and confide in you.

CHAPTER 9

Cast into the Falling Tide

When I was a kid, I was crazy about fishing. Ocean fishing is fun but really different from fishing in a lake. You don't just throw in your line and expect to catch something. The falling tide is when the game fish are stirred up and looking to bite everything. The falling tide of your life is incredibly scary and difficult.

Seeing it as tragedy can be easier than seeing it as opportunity. Your biggest life transition doesn't have to be a crisis or period of loss. It can be an exciting adventure full of opportunities you never knew existed. The Buddha taught that to be at peace, we must accept the impermanence of life and existence. Even collective transitions on the scale of the coronavirus pandemic are normal and regular.

Liminality between the phases of adult life is especially uncomfortable because one doesn't know oneself anymore. The former president of a think tank, he walked away from the people and job he knew and loved to pursue a career as a writer. Bob Greene: Difficult, painful transitions can yield the greatest understanding of purpose in our lives. He says research shows we need periods of pain and struggle that make us temporarily unhappy. Greene: Paradoxically, suffering during transitions can create the meaning in life that imposes a sense of stability.

Does it have to be a "crisis"?

Gail Sheehy's Passages: Predictable Crises of Adult Life sold five million copies. She argued that people naturally go into a midlife crisis at about the age of 40. John DeLorean reacted by divorcing his wife and marrying a twenty-year-old, divorcing her three years later. The term "midlife crisis" was coined by the psychiatrist Elliott Jaques in the 1960s. Research has shown that midlife transitions are real and inevitable, but not always bad.

When we are making a professional reset, we enter liminality. We sense the decline in our intelligence and that we need a change. A major inflection in your life doesn't mean you will abandon your spouse or buy a sports car. Instead, it can bring you closer to your family and friends and inspire others. Bob Greene: My grandfather was the anti-DeLorean; he asked for work and found a new career path.

His father followed in his footsteps and earned a PhD in biostatistics. Greene: Career reset doesn't have to result in midlife crisis like John DeLorean's did. Eight hundred participants have come from many walks of life. They aim to reset their lives in a way that they can serve others with their ideas and experience. There are four learning steps in becoming a "modern elder".

What activities will you keep and what will you evolve and do differently? Chip calls this "the next charter of your life," and it features a number of similarities to lessons learned in previous chapters. A reset at fifty is hardly late in life, Chip says.

Four lessons for a good liminality

Here are some concrete lessons to get started, based on the best research and most successful strategies I have seen.

LESSON 1: IDENTIFY YOUR MARSHMALLOW

The marshmallow test is a classic social-science experiment. Good things come to those who wait, and work, and sacrifice, and maybe even suffer. Read on for the next three lessons in my new book, What Is The Next Marshmallow?

LESSON 2: THE WORK YOU DO HAS TO BE THE REWARD

Whether it's money, power, prestige or prestige, the instrumentalization of work leads to unhappiness. With the right goals, you can make the rest of your career itself your reward. Your reset won't give you joy and fulfillment every day, like anything else in life.

LESSON 3: DO THE MOST INTERESTING THING YOU CAN

In the quest for the professional marshmallow, I think we should seek work that is a balance of enjoyable and meaningful. Interest is considered by many neuroscientists to be a positive primary emotion, processed in the limbic system of the brain. Something that truly interests you is intensely pleasurable; it also must have meaning.

LESSON 4: A CAREER CHANGE DOESN'T HAVE TO BE A STRAIGHT LINE

Scholars have studied career patterns and come up with four broad categories. Spiral careers are more like a series of mini careers. Steady-state careers involve staying at one job and growing in expertise. Transitory careers are ones in which people jump from job to job or field to field, looking for new challenges. In Tibetan Buddhism there is a concept called "bardo," which is a state of existence between death and rebirth. Before you do it, quitting feels like standing at the edge of a cliff, unsure whether what awaits will bring pleasure or pain—or, most likely, both.

CONCLUSION

Seven Words to Remember

Paul Waldman's new book argues that we must fight our natural instincts if we want to be happy. We need to adopt a new formula, which he lays out in detail in this book, chapter by chapter. But of course you are unlikely to memorize the last sixty thousand words. I am not exhorting you to hate and reject the world; to live like a hermit in a Himalayan cave. There is nothing bad or shameful about the world's material abundance, and we are right to enjoy it.

Love is reserved for people, not things; to misplace your love invites frustration and futility. After the 9/11 terrorist attacks, many of you asked what happened to the man on the plane.